REVISION

To begin with, here are some exercises from Book Fu
The WORD LIST at the end of the book will help
Join together words like does *and* not, did *and* not

1. Father does not like cutting the grass.

....

2. I did not understand what he said.

....

3. They are on the top shelf.

....

4. We are going out on Saturday.

....

Rewrite each sentence so that it ends with the words in italics.

5. *The two boys* climbed over the wall.

....

6. *Back to its nest* flew the bird.

....

7. *The baby* sat in its pram.

....

8. Sitting *on the doorstep* was a small puppy.

....

Fill in the spaces with suitable adjectives (describing words).

9. The .... car couldn't climb the .... hill.

10. It took three .... men to lift the .... box.

11. The .... boy could reach the .... shelf.

12. The .... sun soon dried the .... grass.

THE ALPHABET

Write the letters of the alphabet in the spaces provided and against each letter write two words beginning with that letter. Choose words from this list, putting capital letters where necessary.

cheese	geese	ocean	x-rays	machine
wheel	pastry	july	easter	zion
elm	answer	journey	radio	scotland
library	norman	warwick	cardiff	umbrella
vinegar	bank	monday	tennis	neighbour
belfast	kate	kitchen	preston	xylophone
russia	uranus	trevor	france	queensland
oxford	herald	island	leeds	yvonne
desert	david	ireland	zinc	sardine
fence	question	venus	helen	australia
	glasgow		yacht	

A ....

B ....

C ....

....

....

....

....

....

....

....

.... X ....

.... Y ....

.... Z ....

ALPHABETICAL ORDER (1)

Here are ten short lists of words. Arrange each one in alphabetical order.

A   B   C   D   E   F   G   H   I   J   K   L   M
N   O   P   Q   R   S   T   U   V   W   X   Y   Z

1. furniture ....
   people ....
   dress ....
   event ....
   Monday ....

2. hose ....
   change ....
   rabbit ....
   forget ....
   arrange ....

3. decide ....
   arrange ....
   drink ....

4. forget ....
   measure ....
   find ....

5. man ....
   number ....
   men ....

6. whistle ....
   weather ....
   watch ....

7. goose ....
   biscuit ....
   ball ....
   geese ....

8. web ....
   valley ....
   window ....
   water ....

9. teach ....
   time ....
   turn ....
   take ....

10. pay ....
    peach ....
    pond ....
    play ....

3

ALPHABETICAL ORDER   (2)

Here are eight more lists of words.   Arrange each one in alphabetical order.

1. daisy   ....
    brain   ....
    chair   ....
    cat   ....
    ceiling   ....

2. hit   ....
    joke   ....
    hundred   ....
    hand   ....
    hart   ....

3. minute   ....
    measure   ....
    letter   ....
    matter   ....
    language   ....

4. defeat   ....
    electricity   ....
    dragon   ....
    door   ....
    entrance   ....

5. cabbage   ....
    cinder   ....
    centre   ....
    cover   ....
    cloud   ....

6. trap   ....
    tender   ....
    tap   ....
    tunnel   ....
    tiger   ....

7. arrival   ....
    actor   ....
    air   ....
    departure   ....
    answer   ....

8. loop   ....
    luck   ....
    leaf   ....
    liver   ....
    lamb   ....

CAPITAL LETTERS

Rewrite the sentences, putting in capital letters where necessary.

1. the boys were playing football.

   ....

2. david brookes lives next door.

   ....

3. my uncle john has a big dog.

   ....

4. i enjoyed reading *treasure island*.

   ....

5. it was written by r l stevenson.

   ....

6. the programme was on bbc television.

   ....

7. the passengers boarded the liner *queen elizabeth*.

   ....

8. marion was absent on monday.

   ....

9. autumn begins in september.

   ....

10. the first king of england and scotland was james I.

    ....

11. the shop is in high street.

    ....

12. i saw mr davis in his garden.

    ....

COMPLETE THE SENTENCES

do   does

1. Malcolm .... not like cricket.

2. I .... not think it will rain.

3. Derek always .... his best.

4. The dog .... not like strangers.

5. We .... not go to school every day.

6. These shoes .... not fit me.

7. Gerald .... not write very often.

did   done

8. Jane has .... well at school.

9. We .... Exercise 12 last week.

10. I .... not think it would rain.

11. We have .... all we can.

12. Raymond .... his homework upstairs.

13. "Who .... that?" the man asked.

14. "Has she .... her work?" I asked.

seen   saw

15. One of us .... him this morning.

16. We .... the house last week.

17. Has any one .... my football shorts?

18. No, I have not .... them.

19. He had never .... a snake before.

20. She .... the doctor yesterday.

6

RE-ARRANGING SENTENCES

Rewrite each sentence, putting the words in a different order.

1. We were pleased when the sun came out.

   When the sun came out we were pleased
   ....

2. The soil at the edge of the garden was dry.

   ....

3. Over there is our playing field.

   ....

4. I am going home at four o'clock.

   ....

5. An electric clock stands on the cupboard.

   ....

6. I shall write to my uncle to-morrow.

   ....

7. The little boy dashed across the road.

   ....

8. "I often go there," said Sylvia.

   ....

9. Red is the colour of the Merchant Navy flag.

   ....

10. Wide is the opposite of narrow.

    ....

11. Madrid is the capital of Spain.

    ....

12. Over the hurdles jumped the athletes.

    ....

REWRITING SENTENCES   (1)

Rewrite the sentences in the way shown in this example:

Geoffrey broke his pencil.
Geoffrey has broken his pencil.

1. Mr Ford took the money to the bank.

   ....

2. Gillian tore her new dress.

   ....

3. Keith did all his homework.

   ....

4. She ate all her dinner.

   ....

5. I wrote a letter to my uncle.

   ....

6. Edward broke the kitchen window.

   ....

7. I saw Mr Hart's new car.

   ....

8. Mrs White rang the bell.

   ....

9. The referee blew his whistle.

   ....

10. Mother forgot to take her umbrella.

    ....

11. The dog bit the little girl.

    ....

REWRITING SENTENCES (2)

Rewrite the sentences in the way shown in this example:

> Peter swam across the swimming bath.
> Peter has swum across the swimming bath.

1. The workmen began to mend the road.

   ....

2. The children went to the pantomime.

   ....

3. The boat sprang a leak.

   ....

4. The birds flew away.

   ....

5. Mother gave me some money to spend.

   ....

6. I knew about it all the time.

   ....

7. Judith fell off the swing.

   ....

8. David swam across the river.

   ....

9. The destroyer sank the torpedo boat.

   ....

10. The lady wore the same coat for many years.

    ....

11. Jack ran all the way to school.

    ....

REWRITING SENTENCES   (3)

Rewrite the sentences in the way shown in this example:

The goalkeeper threw the ball.
The ball was thrown by the goalkeeper.

1. The Romans built the aqueduct.

   ....

2. The thief stole the bicycle.

   ....

3. The choir sang three songs.

   ....

4. The ball broke the window.

   ....

5. Lesley drew the picture.

   ....

6. The dog bit the little girl.

   ....

7. The wind blew the fence down.

   ....

8. Mrs White rang the bell.

   ....

9. The world champion drove the car.

   ....

10. The pilot flew the aeroplane.

    ....

11. The sound of thunder awoke the children.

    ....

REWRITING SENTENCES (4)

Rewrite the sentences in the way shown in this example:

Susan is a graceful dancer.
Susan dances gracefully.

1. My sister is a careful worker.

   ....

2. The soldiers were brave fighters.

   ....

3. The mayor made a brief speech.

   ....

4. We approached in silence.

   ....

5. The king was a wise ruler.

   ....

6. We made slow progress up the steep hill.

   ....

7. The army made a hasty withdrawal.

   ....

8. We were defeated by a narrow margin.

   ....

9. Their dog is a greedy eater.

   ....

10. The baby is a sound sleeper.

    ....

11. The workmen made a vigorous protest.

    ....

SENTENCES

Re-arrange these mixed-up groups of words into sentences:

1.	The boys	collects the eggs every day.
2.	Graham Smith	were kept in the kitchen.
3.	The blackbird	were playing football.
4.	The kittens	were built in 1964.
5.	The big mallet	are very fond of knitting.
6.	The knives and forks	is captain of the football team.
7.	The garage	has a long handle.
8.	The houses	perched on top of the wall.
9.	The farmer's wife	was built at the side of the house.
10.	My sisters	like to play with a ball of string.

1. *The boys* ....

2. *Graham Smith* ....

3. ....

....

4. ....

....

5. ....

6. ....

....

7. ....

....

8. ....

9. ....

....

10. ....

PEOPLE AT WORK

Write two sentences about each of these people. First say where each person works and then say something about the work they do.

1. I am a chef.

   I work in the kitchen of a hotel or restaurant
   ....

   I cook food for people to eat
   ....

2. I am a waiter.

   ....

   ....

3. I am a clown.

   ....

   ....

4. I am a librarian.

   ....

   ....

5. I am a secretary.

   ....

   ....

6. I am a shopkeeper.

   ....

   ....

7. I am a teacher.

   ....

   ....

13

MADE OF AND USED FOR

A. *Write five sentences (one for each) to say what these things are made of:* 1. windows 2. cricket bats 3. bread 4. butter 5. jerseys

1. ....

2. ....

3. ....

4. ....

5. ....

B. *Write five sentences (one for each) to say what these things are used for:* 6. a pen 7. coal 8. a needle 9. an axe 10. a spade

6. ....

7. ....

8. ....

9. ....

10. ....

C. *Write six sentences (two for each) to say what these things are made of and used for:* 11, 12. chairs 13, 14. knives 15, 16. wine

11. ....

12. ....

13. ....

14. ....

15. ....

16. ....

THE HIGHWAYMAN

Many years ago, a stage-coach was travelling from Bath to London when a masked highwayman suddenly appeared from behind a clump of trees. He brandished his pistol menacingly and demanded that the coach should stop. The driver obeyed instantly and pulled on his reins to stop the horses. The highwayman then opened the coach door and ordered the passengers to surrender their money and other valuables. One man handed over his wallet which contained £50. The highwayman took out the money and returned the wallet to its owner.

At last, when everyone had been robbed, the stage-coach was allowed to continue. Most of the passengers were very distressed, but the man who had handed over his wallet did not feel too badly. True enough, he had lost £50, but he had another £500 in a box under the seat.

1. Did this happen recently or a long time ago?

    ....

2. What did highwaymen do?

    ....

3. Why did highwaymen wear masks?

    ....

4. Where was the coach travelling?

    ....

5. Where had the highwayman been hiding?

    ....

6. What did the highwayman demand?

    ....

7. What did the driver do?

    ....

8. What did the highwayman order the passengers to do?

    ....

9. Why did the man not feel too badly about losing £50?

    ....

ONE WORD FOR SEVERAL

Rewrite the sentences, replacing the words in italics by one word.

1. We put our *cases and bags* on the rack.

   ....

2. The *way out* was clearly marked.

   ....

3. The *room at the top of the house* was full of lumber.

   ....

4. There was a long *line of people* outside the theatre.

   ....

5. We rode as far as the *end of the bus route*.

   ....

6. The programme began at *twelve o'clock midday*.

   ....

7. Rome is the *chief city* of Italy.

   ....

8. The *man who plays in goal* is very tall.

   ....

9. We waited in the *passage-way outside the classrooms*.

   ....

10. My *father's father* lives in Wales.

    ....

11. The *outline of the concert* cost me ten pence

    ....

12. The *people taking part in the competition* waited at the side.

    ....

SINGULAR AND PLURAL (1)

Rewrite the sentences, changing the word in brackets to mean more than one thing or person.

1. The dentist looked at my (tooth).

   ....

2. The (workman) dug a hole in the road.

   ....

3. The (mouse) ate the cheese.

   ....

4. I placed the (mouse-trap) on the floor.

   ....

5. The (lady-in-waiting) helped the queen.

   ....

6. The (commander-in-chief) met to discuss plans.

   ....

7. Several (coat of arms) were hung on the walls.

   ....

8. The (half-back) played a good game.

   ....

9. The (passer-by) stopped to have a look.

   ....

10. I put three (spoonful) of tea in the pot.

    ....

11. She put two (cupful) of flour in the bowl.

    ....

12. We saw the (salmon) in the river.

    ....

SINGULAR AND PLURAL (2)

Write these sentences in the plural:

1. The foreman gave the order.

   ....

2. The woman looked after the goose.

   ....

3. The policeman stopped the bus.

   ....

4. The fireman used an axe.

   ....

5. The postman was delivering letters.

   ....

6. Jack's foot was wet.

   ....

7. The farmer found his sheep.

   ....

8. The window-cleaner has been to-day.

   ....

9. The office boy took the message.

   ....

10. A warship is sometimes called a man-of-war.

    ....

11. I could see the cliff in the distance.

    ....

12. The thief wore a mask.

    ....

PLURALS

Write down the plurals of these words:

1. deer ....
2. salmon ....
3. species ....
4. sheep ....
5. trout ....
6. dozen ....
7. grouse ....

8. cod ....
9. landlady ....
10. housewife ....
11. prince ....
12. princess ....
13. handful ....
14. floorcloth ....

15. window-cleaner ....
16. office boy ....
17. step-mother ....
18. step-father ....
19. major-general ....
20. governor-general ....
21. page-boy ....
22. police constable ....
23. lawnmower ....
24. prize-winner ....
25. maid of honour ....
26. father-in-law ....
27. mother-in-law ....
28. son-in-law ....

MASCULINE—FEMININE

Write down the feminine of these words:

1. man ....
2. boy ....
3. husband ....
4. uncle ....
5. grandfather ....
6. nephew ....
7. son ....
8. brother ....
9. father ....
10. king ....
11. prince ....
12. duke ....
13. lord ....
14. emperor ....
15. actor ....
16. bull ....
17. host ....
18. landlord ....
19. waiter ....
20. gander ....
21. master ....

22. count ....
23. author ....
24. hero ....
25. policeman ....
26. abbot ....
27. horse ....
28. shepherd ....
29. mayor ....
30. lad ....
31. tailor ....
32. grandson ....
33. dog ....
34. sir ....
35. heir ....
36. wizard ....
37. baron ....
38. son-in-law ....
39. gentleman ....
40. headmaster ....
41. drake ....
42. manager ....

ABBREVIATIONS

Write out these abbreviations in full:

1. Ltd
2. Wed.
3. Sat.
4. etc.
5. Rd
6. St
7. Co.
8. No.
9. Dr
10. A.A.
11. R.A.C.
12. B.B.C.
13. M.P.
14. B.C.
15. A.D.
16. R.A.F.
17. R.N.
18. e.g.
19. U.S.A.
20. O.H.M.S.
21. Feb.

JOINING SENTENCES

Join each pair of sentences, using and, but *or* because. (*You may have to miss out one or two words.*)

1. I got into bed.   I went to sleep.

....

2. The shop was open.   There were no customers inside.

....

3. It began to rain.   People ran for shelter.

....

4. People ran for shelter.   It began to rain.

....

5. The food looked delicious.   I wasn't hungry.

....

6. We lost our way.   It was foggy.

....

7. The fire brigade was called.   The fire wasn't serious.

....

8. It was very dark.   I could not find my way.

....

9. The bridge was closed.   It was unsafe.

....

10. The children were punished.   They were sent to bed.

....

11. I used to like tea.   Now I prefer coffee.

....

12. Mother swept the yard.   It was dirty.

....

AND OR BUT

Write two sentences beginning with the words given. Complete the first by adding something beginning with and. *Complete the second by adding a few words beginning with* but.

1. I called for my friend

   I called for my friend and we went to school together
   ....

   I called for my friend but he was not at home
   ....

2. It was a fine day

   ....

   ....

3. She worked carefully

   ....

   ....

4. The tickets were expensive

   ....

   ....

5. The player hurt his foot

   ....

   ....

6. We looked up

   ....

   ....

7. The dog barked

   ....

   ....

WHO AND WHICH

We use who *when we speak about people, and* which *when we speak about things.*
Join each pair of sentences, using who *or* which.   *(Some words may have to be missed out.)*

1. The dormouse is a small animal.
   It goes to sleep during winter.

   ....

2. We played with John's model railway.
   It has always fascinated me.

   ....

3. We asked the policeman.
   He was standing at the corner.

   ....

4. Jack is writing a letter to his sister.
   She is in hospital.

   ....

5. She was looking for her dog.
   It had been missing for several hours.

   ....

6. The crowd applauded the batsman.
   He had scored a century.

   ....

7. The emperor had a wife.
   She was very fond of cats.

   ....

8. We went to the annual fair.
   It attracted a large crowd.

   ....

JOINING WORDS

Join each pair of sentences, using one of these words:

until   and   or

when   where   but

(*Miss out words in italics.*)

1. I sat down. *I* read my book.

....

2. We searched for the ball. *We* couldn't find it.

....

3. You must go at once. You will miss the bus *if you don't.*

....

4. Charles hid in the tree. *He came down when* his pursuers went on their way.

....

5. We looked up at the trees. The rooks were building their nests *there.*

....

Join each pair of sentences, using one of these words:

        as   while   because   although

Then re-arrange each sentence so that it begins with the word chosen from the list.

6. Mother cooked the dinner. Father worked in the garden.

....

....

7. The game continued. The light was poor.

....

....

8. John stayed at home. He had a bad cold.

....

....

WRITE THE NEXT WORD

Write the most suitable word in each space.

1. Boy, Man, Girl, ...

2. Sky, Blue, Grass, ...

3. Spade, Dig, Knife, ...

4. Man, Men, Child, ...

5. Bread, Eat, Milk, ...

6. Pair, Two, Dozen, ...

7. First, January, Second, ...

8. Four, Square, Three, ...

9. Good, Bad, Rich, ...

10. Pear, Pair, Seen, ...

11. Five, Fifth, Eight, ...

12. Four, Quarters, Two, ...

13. Down, Own, Four, ...

14. Six, Sixty, Ten, ...

15. Host, Hostess, Actor, ...

16. Butcher, Meat, Florist, ...

17. Aunt, Uncle, Nephew, ...

18. Evening, Supper, Morning, ...

19. Stairs, Steps, Ladder, ...

20. Bedroom, Sleep, Dining-room, ...

21. Pork, Pig, Mutton, ...

GROUP NAMES

Write a name for each group of words.

1. breakfast, dinner, tea, supper — meal
2. spring, summer, autumn, winter — ....
3. wren, starling, swallow, curlew — ....
4. plane, ash, alder, pine — ....
5. tea, coffee, lemonade, wine — ....
6. bread, meat, vegetable, fruit — ....
7. coat, dress, shirt, stockings — ....
8. tiger, dog, antelope, squirrel — ....
9. March, February, April, November — ....
10. Wednesday, Thursday, Saturday, Sunday — ....
11. two, eight, eleven, seven — ....
12. uncle, cousin, grandfather, aunt — ....
13. tea, lemonade, water, petrol — ....
14. rose, daisy, dandelion, daffodil — ....
15. India, Canada, Mexico, New Zealand — ....
16. football, tennis, cricket, chess — ....
17. salmon, plaice, herring, trout — ....
18. table, chair, cupboard, bed — ....
19. bedroom, lounge, bathroom, kitchen — ....
20. orange, apple, banana, peach — ....
21. carrot, turnip, bean, potato — ....

COMPOUND WORDS

Make new words (such as bodyguard, padlock) *by joining together a word from the left-hand group and a word from the right-hand group.*

body	some	break		paper	word	writer
pad	time	side		all	noon	guard
butter	over	news		table	board	fast
can	wheel	type		barrow	one	side
out	after	pass		lock	fly	not

....

....

....

....

....

PHRASES

Complete these well-known phrases by adding one word:

1. bread and ....

2. lock and ....

3. fish and ....

4. pins and ....

5. brush and ....

6. bucket and ....

7. night and ....

8. high and ....

9. cat and ....

10. thick and ....

11. black and ....

12. time and ....

13. touch and ....

14. safe and ....

15. ways and ....

16. odds and ....

17. spick and ....

18. rough and ....

19. wear and ....

20. heart and ....

WORDS INSTEAD OF NICE

Rewrite these sentences without using the word nice. *Here are some words you may use:*

| comfortable | fine | clever | well-behaved | enjoyable | courteous |
| delicious | fragrant | smart | interesting | refreshing | |

1. Peter is a nice boy.

   ....

2. The peach was nice.

   ....

3. The flowers had a nice smell.

   ....

4. They had nice weather for their holiday.

   ....

5. I had a nice drink of lemonade.

   ....

6. Mrs Green looked very nice in her new dress.

   ....

7. Father has a nice chair at the fireside.

   ....

8. We had a nice holiday last year.

   ....

9. The teacher read a nice story to the class.

   ....

10. Frank thought of a nice idea.

   ....

11. The shopkeeper was always nice to his customers.

   ....

WORDS INSTEAD OF SAID

Rewrite these sentences without using the word said. *Here are some words you may use:*

boasted	asked	concluded	explained
begged	replied	protested	shouted
whispered	suggested	complained	

1. "Is this the train for Manchester?" the lady said.

....

2. "No, madam," the guard said.

....

3. "This is the handbrake," said the instructor.

....

4. "Perhaps you would like this one," said the shop assistant.

....

5. "I am the best player in the school," the boy said.

....

6. "Please, please help me," she said.

....

7. "That is all I have to say," the speaker said.

....

8. "That isn't fair," I said.

....

9. "Stop!" the farmer said, as the man ran away.

....

10. "Don't make a sound," I said.

....

11. "These cakes are stale," the customer said.

....

WORDS INSTEAD OF GOT

Rewrite the sentences without using the word got.   *Here are some words you may use:*

improved	overcame	recovered	mounted
passed	embarked	broke	dismounted
disembarked	avoided	reached	

1. Thieves got into the warehouse during the night.

....

2. The passengers got on the ship at Southampton.

....

3. They got off at New York.

....

4. Mavis got better from tonsilitis.

....

5. The climbers got to the top of the mountain.

....

6. They got over all difficulties.

....

7. Rosemary got through the examination.

....

8. The riders got on their horses.

....

9. After the race, the riders got off.

....

10. The motorist got out of the way of the cyclist.

....

11. His condition got better.

....

WORDS INSTEAD OF WALKED AND PUT

Rewrite the sentences without using the word walked. *Here are some words you can use instead:*

approached	marched	followed
stole	strolled	bumped

1. The soldiers walked smartly along the road.

....

2. The thieves walked off with the jewels.

....

3. The man walked into the lamp post.

....

4. The detective walked behind the man.

....

5. They walked slowly through the park.

....

6. As I walked towards the house, I saw a light.

....

Rewrite these sentences without using the word put:

7. He couldn't put up with the damp climate.

....

8. He had a little money put by.

....

9. We were put out by the bad news.

....

10. The fire brigade put out the fire.

....

11. Several new buildings have been put up.

....

THE HOLE

Some workmen had dug a hole in the middle of the road in order to lay some drainage pipes. When the work was complete the foreman told his men to fill the hole up again while he went for his dinner.

While he was away the men set to work, but they discovered that they couldn't get all the soil and clay back into the hole. This was because the pipes occupied so much space.

When the foreman returned one of his men said to him, "I think we shall have to dig another hole."

"Why?" the foreman asked.

"Well you see," the man explained, "we can't get all the soil back, so we shall have to dig another hole to bury it."

1. Who dug the hole?

   ....

2. Where was the hole?

   ....

3. Why had the hole been dug?

   ....

4. Who told the men to fill the hole up again?

   ....

5. Why did the foreman go away?

   ....

6. What did the men discover?

   ....

7. Why wouldn't all the soil and clay go back into the hole?

   ....

   ....

8. What is a foreman?

   ....

SAME WORD—TWO MEANINGS

Put in a suitable word to finish each sentence. Then write a sentence of your own that includes the word you have just used, but with a different meaning.

1. John hit the ball with his cricket ....

   A bat usually flies at night.
   ....

2. The elephant has a long ....

   ....

3. The man took his money to the ....

   ....

4. He filled his .... with blue ink.

   ....

5. I put a rubber .... round the papers.

   ....

6. The .... were flying at half mast.

   ....

7. Dates grow on .... trees.

   ....

8. I struck a .... when the light went out.

   ....

9. Mother wears a .... on her finger.

   ....

10. The .... would not fit the lock.

    ....

WORDS THAT SOUND ALIKE

Copy out each sentence, choosing the right word from the brackets. Then write a sentence of your own, using the word from the bracket that you did not use to finish the sentence.

1. A fox's (tale, tail) is called a brush.

   A fox's tail is called a brush.

   A tale is a story or fable.

2. A (beach, beech) tree has a grey bark.

3. An (ant, aunt) is an insect.

4. The (boy, buoy) was cleaning his bicycle.

5. They tried to swim against the (current, currant).

6. The child was too (weak, week) to walk.

7. The lion has a (main, mane) on its neck.

MAKING SENTENCES

Use each group of words to make a sentence.

1. saw   lot   people   park

   I saw a lot of people in the park

2. lorry   carrying   bags   coal

3. one   firemen   climbed   ladder

4. young   cat   kitten

5. garden   full   weeds

6. plural   tooth   teeth

7. explorers   looking   source   river

8. hay   used   cattle   winter

9. football   began   three   o'clock

10. coltsfoot   looks   small   dandelion

11. wind   papers   street

12. lighthouse   ships   away   rocks

COMMAS

Use each group of words in a sentence, putting in commas and full stops where necessary.

1. Jane   Mary   Betty   Linda

   I invited Jane, Mary, Betty and Linda to my party
   .

2. blackbirds   thrushes   sparrows   starlings

   .

3. houses   flats   bungalows   shops

   .

4. fruit   jelly   cream   trifle

   .

5. books   pens   pencils   rulers

   .

6. cups   saucers   plates   dishes

   .

7. Arthur   George   Norman   Keith

   .

8. spring   summer   autumn   winter

   .

9. September   April   June   November

   .

10. tea   cocoa   coffee   milk

    .

11. lions   giraffes   bears   monkeys

    .

12. wheat   maize   oats   barley

    .

FINISHING SENTENCES (1)

Write suitable endings to complete the sentences.

1. The concert finished ....
2. The Forth road bridge ....
3. Surrounding the castle ....
4. After tea ....
5. When the storm began ....
6. A large crowd ....
7. We keep the pencils ....
8. The fast car ....
9. A policeman ....
10. Many people ....
11. One of the riders ....
12. My uncle ....
13. Moths ....
14. The twins ....
15. The goalkeeper ....
16. The farmer's wife ....
17. Once a year ....
18. At midnight ....
19. The first question ....
20. Some snakes ....
21. The apple pie ....

FINISHING SENTENCES (2)

Write suitable beginnings to complete the sentences.

1. .... was late for school.

2. .... is closed on Sunday.

3. .... were too big for me.

4. .... buried the bone.

5. ...., is made from flour.

6. .... is the first day of the week.

7. .... next week.

8. .... in the cupboard.

9. .... on the shelf.

10. .... in my pocket.

11. .... at twelve o'clock.

12. .... on my wrist.

13. .... at the side of the house.

14. .... is being widened.

15. .... took three hours.

16. .... injured his leg.

17. .... went to bed early.

18. .... is blue and white.

19. .... blew his whistle.

20. .... bark.

21. .... is twelve years old.

PROVERBS

Try to finish these proverbs.   There is a space for each word.

1. Look before ....

2. Make hay while the ....

3. It's never too late ....

4. Too many cooks spoil ....

5. Two heads are better ....

6. All's well that ....

7. Birds of a feather ....

8. Waste not, ...

9. A stitch in time ....

10. One swallow does not make ....

11. Honesty is the ....

12. A rolling stone gathers ....

13. Once bitten, ...

14. The early bird catches ....

15. A still tongue makes a ....

16. A fool and his money are ....

17. A watched pot ....

18. Rome wasn't built in ....

19. One good turn ....

20. It's a long lane that has ....

21. Don't make a mountain out of ....

APOSTROPHE S

An apostrophe is a raised comma used to show possession:
  the girl's hats means hats belonging to one girl
  the girls' hats means hats belonging to more than one girl

Now rewrite each phrase as shown in the first two.

1. The wings of the butterfly.   *The butterfly's wings.*

2. The wings of the butterflies.   *The butterflies' wings.*

3. The shoes of the boy.

4. The shoes of the boys.

5. The hats of the lady.

6. The hats of the ladies.

7. The captain of the ship.

8. The house of the man.

9. The book of the pupil.

10. The tail of the horse.

11. The tails of the horses.

12. The house of Mr Smith.

13. The secretary of the manager.

14. The wing of the bird.

15. The uniform of the soldier.

16. The uniforms of the soldiers.

17. The helmet of the fireman.

18. The knife of the butcher.

19. The camp of the scouts.

PHRASES

Use each of these phrases in a sentence of your own:

round the corner   next to the house
near the school   once upon a time
early next morning   in his kennel
through the forest   approaching the house
on his bicycle   over the cross-bar
before sunrise   in spite of the fog
in the oven   behind the bushes
out of sight   over the airport

1. ....

2. ....

3. ....

4. ....

5. ....

6. ....

7. ....

8. ....

9. ....

10. ....

11. ....

12. ....

13. ....

14. ....

15. ....

16. ....

EXPLAIN THE DIFFERENCE (1)

Write sentences (one or more) to explain the differences in meaning between each pair of words. If you like, you may first say in which way they are similar and then point out the differences.

1. hymn and song
2. window and mirror
3. house and bungalow
4. crowd and mob
5. road and motorway
6. ceiling and roof

1. *Both hymns and songs are pieces of music to be sung, but whereas a hymn is a song of praise for use in worship, a song can be a setting of any words to music.*

2. ....

....

....

3. ....

....

....

4. ....

....

....

5. ....

....

....

6. ....

....

....

EXPLAIN THE DIFFERENCE (2)

Write sentences (one or more) to explain the differences in meaning between each pair of words. If you like, you may first say in which way they are similar and then point out the differences.

1. crowd and queue
2. desk and table
3. cheer and shout
4. carpet and rug
5. ladder and stairs
6. newspaper and magazine

1. *A crowd is a number of people gathered together in a large group. A queue is a number of people forming a line or column, usually waiting admission to a theatre or stadium.*

2.

3.

4.

5.

6.

44

WORD LIST

abbess
actress
association
attic
authoress
automobile
awakened

bitch
bitten
blown
broken
building

café
calves
capital
children
chosen
circus
comb
competitors
continent
corporation
corridor
court
crowd
cygnet

daughter
doctor
done
drawn
driven
drunk
duchess

eaten
eighth
empress
erected
ewe
exit
extinguished

fallen
February
feet
finished
flown
forgotten
foxes
furniture

given
goalkeeper
gone
goose
grandfather
grown
guilty

halves
heavy
heroine
hidden
hospital

imperfect
index
innocent

known

ladies
language
library
liquid
luggage

mice
monkeys

narrow
niece
noise
noon

ocean
office
operate

palm
parliament
persuaded
policy
programme

queue

restaurant
ridden
route
run
rung

Saturday
scene
school
seen
sewing
shaken

sheltered
sow
spoken
sprung
steel
steep
stolen
strong
sung
sunk
surgery
sword
swum

tailoress
taken
teeth
tent
terminus
theatre
thieves
thrown
tigress
tomatoes
torn
type

vegetable
vixen

waitress
Wednesday
witch
worn
write
writing
written

My Name: _____

My Class : _____

The date I started to use this book:

_____

ISBN 0-17-410256-9

Nelson

I T P

9 780174 102564